MW01193193

Praise for *Transitioning to Retirement: Discovering How to Build Social Networks, Structure and Self-Worth in Retirement*

"Personal stories and insights shared with honesty and empathy. A wise and caring look at the one of the biggest challenges for our lives and for society. Practical, easy to use checklists to help you identify your new normal and write your own ticket.

– Andy Cairns,
Baby Boomer thinking about the next journey.

■ ■ ■

"Retirement is certainly an adjustment and hard work at first. Janet certainly understands this and helps us easily look at our own interests, skills, and greater capabilities. In this book she shows us how to move forward to live productive and enjoyable lives. A must read for those reaching retirement."

– Lois Goldberg,
content retiree.

■ ■ ■

"*Transitioning to Retirement* is a thought-provoking and relevant book for anyone even *thinking* about retirement. Although my 'retirement' is realistically at least 10 years away, this book has changed my outlook already. Author Isaacman astutely draws the parallel that successful retirement, as in any change or transition, depends on planning beyond just financial considerations. She helps the reader imagine the possibilities of this exciting transition beyond the conventional connotation of 'retirement.'"

– M. Rhein,
Baby Boomer

"I really enjoyed reading this book. The writing is accessible, entertainingly anecdotal, positive and provides clear and helpful information. The development of skills and knowledge for personal satisfaction do not end after retirement. This book can help you to find formal and informal fulfillment opportunities all around you.

Susan Woitte, Faculty, Northeastern University

■ ■ ■

"So much attention is paid these days to whether a person is financially ready to retire, but little thought is given to whether a person is _emotionally_ ready. This book does just that. From the author's stories relating her own retirement journey to tales of countless retirees she's interviewed, the reader will learn about many retirement styles and gain the tools to decide which style is right."

– Carol A. Klann
retirement consultant

■ ■ ■

"In the U.S., we have a sophisticated 'retirement planning' industry, complete with advisors and financial products. On reaching retirement, the new retiree often finds that he/she is woefully unprepared to spend wisely the most valuable asset he/she owns – the time to pursue the activities that most fulfill him. It is critical that a retiree utilize a well developed process to identify those activities that will generate the highest return on this most valuable asset. Janet's approach is a logical and easy way to identify one's most fulfilling activities."

– Paul Manghera
CFP; and Mike Neuses, CFA, financial advisors,
Morgan Stanley Smith Barney, Chicago

Transitioning to Retirement

Discovering a New Approach
to Self-Worth, Structure and
Building a Social Network in Retirement

Janet Isaacman

A personal note...

Nothing is more important to me then my family; my loving husband Ted, daughters Susan and Carol, their husbands Gregg and Larry, my sister Karen, and my beloved granddaughters Jessica and Allison. Whether it's a celebration or a difficult situation, they are always at my side providing unconditional love and support.

A special thank you to Dru Sefton and Mary Bender for their professional skills. They brought professionalism to the words of an amateur author.

Finally, yet importantly, I wish to express gratitude to my dear friends, Kelli Schulte and Mark Rhein, for their support throughout the development of this book. They not only provided valuable guidance and advice, they also provided motivation and renewed my inspiration whenever I began to lose faith in the project and threatened to quit.

Table of Contents

Part 1: My Story

Part 2: Your Story

Appendix

I think that there are a lot of people who are really gifted, but never go beyond that one place they see themselves.

It's not until you've gone through all phases of life that you can fully understand the meaning of your gifts.

They are facets of seeing your own self, your own heart and your own mind.

– Delmar Boni
Native American
Artist, Apache Tribe 1996

Foreword

"Janet, why are you trying so hard to find something challenging to do? You've earned the right to retire and take it easy. You worked hard for so many years and achieved so much. It's time to relax!"

Paige, a supervisor in my department, did come to understand my desire to do more than sit in the rocking chair.

She understood what I was feeling when I explained, "Just because I stopped going to work every day doesn't mean that I want to take it easy. I find that I still need the stimulation and satisfaction that I experienced while I was working."

I went on to explain, "I have already lived five more years than my parents did. I enjoy good health and I have the financial means to meet my rather conservative needs. I am old enough to have life figured out and yet young enough to live it!"

"Retirement is a gift," I continued. "You don't know how long this gift will last. My goal is to, while I *can*, make the most of this special time of life.

"So, Paige," I said, "while I can, I will. While I can, I'll do!"

"All of life is an experiment. The more experiments you make the better."

-Ralph Waldo Emerson

PART 1 | MY STORY

Retirement...A Crossroad in My Life.

This is my story. Mine alone.

No one else may fit exactly into the notches I've found in my post-working life, and no one but me may have found their way exactly as I did. But based on conversations I have had with many retirees, some parts of the process I went through are universal.

So, what I am attempting here is to formulate a method that retirees and near-retirees can try, in whole or in part, that will help them find a comfortable and meaningful post-work life known as retirement. I am not offering solutions; I am offering a way you can find your own solutions.

First, let me, by way of introduction, explain who I am and how I came to develop and follow this plan.

I'm in the middle. I am part of the Veteran's Generation (those born between 1925-1945) and fairly close in age to the Baby Boomers. Most of my career I worked with Baby Boomers and I have adopted many of their values and work ethics.

When large numbers of ambitious Baby Boomers joined the workforce, they competed with each other for the decreasing number of available promotions caused by business consolidations. They thought they could get ahead if they worked 12 hours a day and made work their major focus. Their work often defined who they were.

Having lived this work ethic – "If I work hard, I will achieve" – a large percentage of the Baby Boomers do not see themselves enjoying a retirement totally focused on leisure activities.

Some talk about finding a part-time job. Others hope to use their business knowledge and skills to do meaningful work by volunteering to share the expertise they have gained over the years with a nonprofit organization.

One retiree I talked to said that he had a "bucket list" of things he wanted to do before he was too old. To his surprise, the list never shrank. Each year of retirement brought new experiences which led to new items to be added to his ever growing "bucket list."

Some plan to retrain or go through a formal education program that will offer them a second career that would be very different from the career they left.

While some retirees wanted to extend their careers in novel ways, others had to use their retirement to earn money. They chose to take a job where they accepted a lower salary in exchange for less responsibility.

Many of the Baby Boomers look forward to retirement as a time to explore and develop their passions. Articles have been written about business people who follow through on their passions and unfulfilled dreams such as becoming authors, sculptors, mountain climbers. The list goes on.

One Baby Boomer I know loves books and hopes to work in a bookstore. Another friend loves crafts and plans to get a job in a craft store.

While the Baby Boomers I have talked to have a variety of thoughts about retirement, many share a common opinion: They do not want "retirement" as defined by their parents. Their vision of retirement is not living in a mature adults community spending most of their time on the golf course or tennis court.

Some talk about traveling, reading more and maintaining a healthy lifestyle, but they also want a focus that will provide them with the same rewards and meaning that work did.

With a renewed focus on service, many see retirement as an opportunity to give back to society. Whether volunteering, or having a paid job with a nonprofit organization, future retirees see this as a time of life to help others.

Like the Baby Boomers I talked to, I want to get involved in leisure type activities, but also like them, I want to find activities that will bring me the gratifying life that work gave me.

I have discovered that in retirement, it may seem that time is not important; on a daily basis the minutes and how you spend them don't seem to mean much. But how those minutes add up is very important. We don't know how long our retirement will last, how long we will live, how long our health will not be a factor in our decisions of how to spend our time. We need to seize the time.

1. RETIREMENT - A MAJOR LIFE CHANGING EVENT

> Continuity gives us roots; change gives us branches, letting us stretch and grow and reach new heights.
>
> — Pauline R. Keger

Five Months Before Retirement.

"I can't wait until I retire! Its going to be great! I've put together a solid nest egg, and the financial planner tells me it's time to start enjoying!"

TV ads…articles in magazines…stories from those already retired …websites…flyers that come in the mail all focus on this wonderful time of life….RETIREMENT.

The "Golden Years"…a time to reward myself for all the hours I put into my career….all the sacrifices I made to have a successful career.

A chance to move from all the long and stressful workdays to a life of carefree fun.

"I can't wait to read the books I haven't had time to read…*I am going to* learn how to play golf …*I am going to* do more entertaining…*I am going to* do things I love to do, but didn't have time to do because of the demands of my job. *I am going to*…"

■ I'M RETIRED! HONOR THE PAST...CELEBRATE THE END...PLAN THE FUTURE

Retirement + One Day

"Okay. I did it. I packed up my office, had a retirement party, popped the balloons, shook hands and said my goodbyes. Now what?"

I chose to walk away from my job at the top of my game, so I continued to work at a torrid pace until just a couple of days before I retired. I scheduled meetings and maintained my level of interest and serious involvement until the week before retirement.

But the day after I retired, I woke up and realized that I had nothing to do, no meetings to attend, no aggressive deadlines to meet, no projects to complete, no staff issues. Nobody was expecting anything from me. Only 24 hours before I had been pulled in so many directions as requests for actions and answers came nonstop from employees, peers and bosses.

In one day I had gone from the stress and challenges of being a leader in a large corporation to zero expectations. Nobody was wanting or waiting for anything from me.

As I lay in bed the morning after the retirement party, it hit me. As someone who had worked since she was 16 years old, I was about to go through a major change in my life. I was facing a life where work would no longer be a major focus.

■ WHAT'S NEXT?

Retirement Day + Six Months: A Time for Decompression

Before I retired, I developed a transition plan. Still thinking with my "business hat" on, my plan consisted of three goals:

- Short-term: Design a "celebration" to honor the past and begin the future.

- Mid-term: Find activities that would make the first year of retirement enjoyable.

- Long-term: Begin the process of identifying activities to build a rewarding retirement.

Short-Term Goal

My husband and I decided to make the first week after my retirement a week of celebration. On Monday, we had a leisurely breakfast and took the train into the city. Our slow-paced walk to the museum allowed us to take in the sights and sounds of the city. After the museum, we did some window shopping before we had a delicious dinner in a very special restaurant. There was no reason to hurry, and I didn't have to check in with the office to see if anything had come up that required attention. There would be no email or text messages to be reviewed.

On the train ride home, we both agreed that this is good. Before retirement, a day off from work meant it was a day to rest or catch up on chores. But in retirement, there would be time to enjoy places and events that we had not been able to take advantage of while working.

Mid-Term Goal

I like working on projects, so I identified several I could work on during the next few months. Since I had not lost my "business hat," I created informal project plans complete with goals and due dates:

- Modify living quarters. Retirement means spending more time at home so we made changes that would allow our surroundings to better meet our needs. We reduced clutter and gave away items that we no longer needed. We created a new home-theater system and made other purchases that reflected our new lifestyle.

- Clean out shoeboxes filled with pictures that covered four plus generations. Photos were sorted and those to be saved were scanned.

- Transfer videos to CDs.

Long-Term Goal

Along with my home projects, I began to ponder and explore options for the long term. I considered looking for opportunities to work with children and registered for a storytelling class. I also began to write a children's book based on a family story.

My husband and I also decided to take two major vacations a year and prioritized our destinations.

Retirement Day + One Year: A Time for Evaluation

As the one-year anniversary of my retirement approached, I was still excited and felt very positive about this special time of life. I continued to make plans for how I could fill my hours and days with all the things I had thought about during the years leading up to retirement.

- I was making a dent in my "must read" list.

- I was having lunch dates with friends.

- I took a class in a special area of interest.

- I returned to some of the hobbies I had enjoyed but didn't have time to do while I was working.

- I was building some structure, such as making sure I exercised every morning.

In the workplace, I was a focused multitasker; in retirement, I found that I could stay more focused on one activity without getting distracted. But the simple structure I had built was not sufficient. I was beginning to sense that although the life I was enjoying was great for the first year of retirement, I was going to need something more to satisfy me in the long run.

I was beginning to ask, "Is there more? What else do I want to accomplish during this wonderful time of life when I have all this freedom? What can I do to make sure I have a gratifying retirement?"

I realized I needed more than just keeping myself busy.

2. RETIREMENT

The purpose of life is a life of purpose.

- Robert Byrne

THE REST OF MY LIFE

My next step was to think about how my first year of retirement went. How had life changed? How was I spending my time? Did I like what I was doing? Was retirement what I thought it would be? Do I feel fulfilled and satisfied with how I am spending my time? If someone asked me if I like retirement better than working, what would I say?

A Really Big Change

About a year after I retired I realized I was going through one of the biggest changes in my life. It was on a level of when I went away to college, or got married or became a parent.

The "normal" I had known was gone. All the comings and goings of who I was and what I experienced in the workplace were gone.

I was forced to deal with a great deal of uncertainty. I missed the comfort that came with the predictability of my life.

Seeking the New Normal

Some days I feel nervous and scared and wish I had it all figured out. I want someone to come and just tell me what would be good for me, to tell me what kinds of things I could do to be happy, how I should spend my retirement years.

When doubts started to creep in, I stopped and reminded myself that retirement is a gift. It is a time I have been given to focus on me and what would make me happy. There is no "due date." I don't have to meet someone else's expectations. I don't have to report my results to anyone. If I want to change what I am doing, I can do it without asking permission.

As I talked to other retirees, I realized that there is *no one way* to have a successful retirement. Everyone has to create their own personal and satisfying retirement.

Kaizen is the Japanese word for improvement. It represents a philosophy of continual assessment and improvement.

A business never develops a business strategy and then says, "Great. We're done. We've achieved our strategy." Successful businesses follow the Kaizen philosophy and continue to make modifications based on changing business conditions in order to have continued success. - or sometimes even change their strategy.

I have found that the more I experience different activities, the more I change my thinking about what it will take for me to have a meaningful retirement. As I meet new people and try new things, exciting possibilities continue to surface.

One of the activities I had in my initial plan was to be a storyteller. I took a class and joined a group of storytellers. However, other opportunities have presented themselves and for now, I have chosen to postpone entering the world of storytelling. I plan to go back to it at some point, but I have made a conscious decision to modify my priorities.

My first volunteering experience was clerical work for a nonprofit organization, which I thought would be perfect for someone coming out of a demanding work experience. However, after a year, I began to look for a volunteer opportunity that would require more responsibility and make better use of my skills.

Like in a business, I needed to make the process of planning, experiencing, assessing and modifying an ongoing activity. I needed to be patient and make changes as necessary to ensure that I am as satisfied in retirement as I was when I was in the workplace.

Not As Easy As It Looks

I underestimated the difference between having my work determine what I do in a day versus trying to fill my day with meaningful activities.

While I was employed, it was not difficult to find things to do in my spare time. Filling up a few hours on the weekend, or coming up with a dream vacation was one thing, but trying to stay busy all the days and evenings for the rest of my life was quite another!

Until I had an empty schedule in front of me, I didn't fully understand what it would take to create a worthwhile retirement, how I could spend this very special gift of time.

Other retirees I talked to shared my challenge. When they retired, they thought enjoying favorite activities such as golfing would be satisfying. They reported that after about a year, there was such a thing as too much golf.

Most of the retirees reported that they had no trouble "keeping busy." They belonged to book clubs, traveled, attended classes, had hobbies, met friends for lunch and participated in sports. But somewhere after a year of retirement, they realized that spending time doing a variety of unconnected activities was not going to be satisfying in the long term.

So while I, as well as many other retirees, agreed that we loved retirement and did not want the pressures of the workplace, there were some things about work that we missed.

■ WHAT'S MISSING?

I gave a great deal of thought as to what I missed by not being in the workplace. What were the good things about working? What gave me a feeling of satisfaction? What kinds of things made me feel good about what I was doing? I concluded that there were three key elements of the working environment that I missed…I call them the 3 S's.

- Structure
- Social Network
- Self Worth

Then: Workdays were brimming with meetings and deadlines with very little free, unplanned time. My job provided a structure where I usually had a pretty good idea of what was going to happen thorughout the day. As a leader, much of my workday was filled with interacting with others and helping to solve problems and overcome challenges.

Many other retirees said that they had very structured jobs and really missed their work routines. A magazine editor talked about yearning for the emotional high he would get every month as he sent to the printer the completed magazine that was the result of working very hard throughout the month.

Now: While there will be numerous commitments and obligations, for the most part you will have a pretty empty slate. You will be able to decide what you do and when you want to do it.

Some retirees laugh about how much time they waste. How chores that used to take a few minutes are now done at a more leisurely pace and take up more hours per day.

I have done several things to help build structure. I don't want so much structure that I feel like I am in a box, or feel stressed from being overly organized. But I have built some things into my life that help create, for me, the right amount of structure.

For example, on Sundays I always clean the pile of papers I have accumulated over the week, as well as the emails to which I have not responded. I try to go to sleep and get up at the same time every day. I take a class that meets every Tuesday morning and I exercise most days right after breakfast.

One thing I miss in retirement is "the weekend." The talk in the workplace on a Friday centered around the weekend activities. People looked forward to the change of pace and spending time doing the things they liked to do.

In retirement, there is no such "Friday." So I have built, for myself, a week and a weekend. During the week I have a set of routines that are different from the ones I have on the weekend. During the week I spend time with friends, attending events or doing volunteer work. The weekend is spent doing things with my husband. This includes leisurely brunches on Saturday and Sunday mornings.

Then: Time in the office was filled with all kinds of social opportunities. In addition to formal meetings, there were times when my staff and peers would stop by throughout the day to share experiences or have a good laugh. The lunch hour was an opportunity to keep up with friends in other departments.

Now: In retirement, I feel like I need a social secretary. If I don't arrange social engagements or make plans to participate in events, I am looking at an empty calendar – a week with no social interactions.

Then: I have many memories of times when I left work at the end of the day feeling good about my contributions. Even for those who did not love their job, over the years the workplace provided opportunities to make a difference: To have a positive impact on the business, customers and the people they worked with.

Based on my contributions, I had a sense of my own value as a person. My work gave me a sense of identification.

There were activities and events that energized me and provided me with intellectual and emotional fulfillment.

Life had an "edge" – excitement and energy provided by deadlines and never-ending work.

Now: The biggest challenge in retirement has been to find a way to regain self-worth. Reading, learning how to play golf and spending time with friends was enjoyable, but did nothing to make me feel good about how I was contributing to making something or someone better.

Volunteering has been the path I have taken to rebuild my self-worth.

■ REPLACING WORKPLACE REWARDS IN RETIREMENT

I am in my sixth year of retirement and I continue to work on creating **Structure** to fill my open days, weeks and months. I continue to work on building a **Social** network...and finding activities that provide me with **Self-worth** and fill my need to make a difference. I continue to make sure that I am intellectually and emotionally fulfilled.

PART 2 | YOUR STORY

The rest of this book will contain Your Story! It provides a process and tools to help you build a satisfying and fulfilling retirement.

Whether you are retired or are thinking about it, this will help you start to build an unique retirement journey that will give you a feeling of satisfaction and fulfillment.

■ FIRST LEG OF THE JOURNEY

First Day of Retirement

Plan a day to celebrate the end of one phase of your life and the beginning of the next phase of your life. Do something you love to do, but didn't have time to do when you were working.

Examples: fishing, visiting a favorite museum, spending time with an out-of-town friend you haven't seen for a while, going to a concert or play, playing golf, visiting grandchildren, dining out at a new and exciting restaurant, or a small, intimate bistro.

■ SECOND LEG OF THE JOURNEY

First Six to 12 Months

Have a list ready of things you like to do that will keep you busy.

Examples: Read. Take a trip to a place you have always wanted to go. Start or return to a hobby that you were once involved with. Take a class. Start to research activities that you could do in retirement.

■ THIRD LEG OF THE JOURNEY

Never-Ending Journey

Identify and participate in activities that will create a long and satisfying retirement.

My interest is in the future because I am going to spend the rest of my life there.

- Charles F. Kettering

■ WHAT KIND OF RETIREMENT LIFESTYLE DO YOU WANT?

The Third Leg of Your Journey

Retirees I have talked to found that how they spent their time in retirement fell into one of three lifestyles.

Joe decided to continue working. He loved electronic equipment and was happy selling technology on a part-time basis for a small entrepreneurial company.

Joe's friend Bill preferred to have an informal schedule that allowed him to make last minute decisions on how he spent his time.

When Joe's other friend Ed retired, he was so excited about being free from the long hours his job required that he just went from one activity to another. However, after a year he decided that he wanted direction in his life. Ed wanted a more predictable lifestyle, so he identified a focus that would give him a more fulfilling and satisfying retirement.

Retirement Lifestyle Options

Informal	Structured	
Activities scheduled on an ad hoc basis. Minimum structure and/or focus.	Focused A plan is developed that ensures an alignment between retirement activities and a feeling of fulfillment and satisfaction.	Work Continuation • Similar work-New Job with new company (full or part time) • Second career – Different area of expertise

■ CREATING A RETIREMENT JOURNEY

When we deal with big events in our lives, we give much thought to available options before making decisions: selection of a college/university, planning a wedding, buying a house, changing careers. We then figure out the actions necessary to actually buy the house or get into the college or university we have chosen.

A process with supporting tools and exercises that can be used and reused throughout retirement is provided on the following pages. The process will help you develop a plan that allows you to be diligent in your approach to retirement instead of letting retirement happen.

The exercises and tools will serve as guide to:

- Creating a Focus: Generating Ideas

- Identifying Activity Paths

- Selecting Activities

- Tracking Progress

- Monitoring Success

STEP 1: COMPLETING A SELF-AUDIT

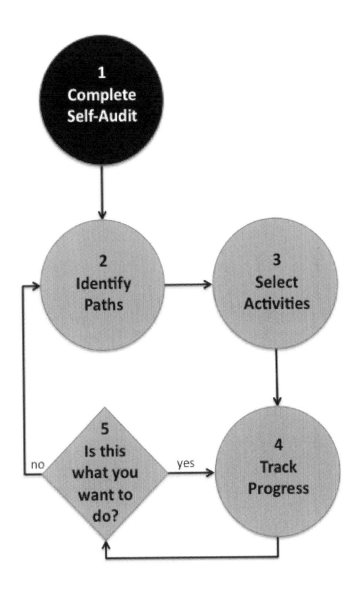

■ STEP 1: COMPLETING A SELF-AUDIT

What About Me

The first step in planning a satisfying retirement is to understand yourself and discover:

- What do you like to do?

- What successes have you enjoyed during your pre-retirement years?

- What are you really good at?

- What is most important to you?

The following section offers probing questions to help you begin the process of identifying activities which will lead to a satisfying retirement.

As you answer the questions, it is important that you examine each thoughtfully and not settle for quick answers.

Say that you like being with people. That is a very broad statement. Does it mean you like to socialize in large groups, or do you prefer to interact with one or two friends at a time? If you like to be part of a group, would you prefer groups that are informal or more formal, where the members have a shared focus such as fundraising for the local hospital? Do you like competitive events? Do you like athletic events? Probing deeper will help provide you with more specific and helpful information.

With the information you gather, you will be able to establish a focus and identify activities that will bring you a satisfying retirement.

SECTION A: Activities in Which You Enjoyed or Excelled

- *During your childhood, what activities did you enjoy? If, as a child you had more free time, how would you have spent your time? Example: team soccer, playing the piano*

....

....

....

....

- *During summer vacations, did you prefer organized activities or did you prefer the freedom to do as you pleased? What kinds of activities did you like to do? Example: puzzles, hiking, did not like camp, preferred unorganized activities*

....

....

....

....

- *During your early adult years, what activities did you enjoy? In what activities did you excel? What skills helped you excel? Example: had a good singing voice, sang in the church choir*

....

....

....

....

- As you experienced middle age and your responsibilities grew, what activities would you have wanted to participate in if you had more free time? Example: learn a new language, master photography, spend more time with family

....

....

....

....

- If you knew in advance that you had one week with no responsibilities, how would you have spent that week? In what types of activities would you have chosen to be involved? Example: take a rafting trip down the Colorado River

....

....

....

....

- Based on what you learned about yourself as you looked back over the years, what activities might you consider doing in retirement?

....

....

....

....

....

SECTION B: Your Career Accomplishments

- *As you review all your work experiences, which jobs did you find the most rewarding? What did you like about those jobs? What did you dislike about those jobs? Example: leader of department, liked developing employees but did not like dealing with poor employee performance*

....

....

....

....

- *What were the two greatest contributions you made during your career? What skills helped you excel? Example: came up with a time savings idea that saved the company over $100,000, good at building efficient and effective systems*

....

....

....

....

- *What types of job activities excited you? Example: business trips, meeting customers outside the US*

....

....

....

....

- *What kinds of activities did you dislike? Example: filling out daily productivity report, meetings*

....

....

....

- *If you think about the feedback you have received over the years, from teachers, friends, bosses and peers, what strengths were consistently identified? Example: working with others, writing skills*

....

....

....

- *As your job responsibilities increased, which responsibilities did you enjoy taking on? Which responsibilities did you not enjoy? Example: liked designing and implementing project plans*

....

....

....

- *What did you learn about yourself as you look back on your career?*

....

....

....

SECTION C: Other Things to Think About

- *Interests: Over the years, what hobbies or groups did you participate in that you enjoyed? Example: volunteer, participating in theater group, cooking*

....

....

- *Interests: Because of job and/or family obligations, were there any interests you did not have time to explore? Example: writing an article for a professional magazine, travel to another country*

....

....

- *Successes: Did you win any honors or prizes? What skills did you use to be a winner? Example: great salesperson, salesperson of the year*

....

....

- *Successes: What were your three greatest accomplishments in life, personal or professional? Example: parenting, remodeling project, presentation at a conference*

....

....

....

....

Place an "x" on the line closest to the activity that best reflects your social preferences.

Prefer to do activities with others	Prefer to do activities alone

Outdoor activities	Indoor activities

Creative activities	Activities that require cognitive thinking and are structured

Maintain social connections with people I knew from work	Not have any connections to the place were I worked

Make new friends	Focus on current friendships

Maintain a small group of close friends	Be part of formal organizations

What did you learn about your social preferences that will help you decide how you want to spend your time?

....

....

....

Values are those things that really matter to us: what we consider highly worthwhile. Everyone has a core set of personal values. Examples are helping those who are in need, being part of an organization that works to improve the environment, eating healthy or donating money to a favorite charity.

Values represent our highest priorities and what drives our decisions and actions.

Values can change over time in response to changing life experiences. The exercise on the next page will help you identify the values that are most important to you at this time of your life. The values you currently hold most dear will impact your decisions about how you want to spend your retirement years.

Refer to the 24 values on the following page. If you wish to expand the list, the Internet can provide you with additional values to review and consider (search on *values*). Place additional values in the blank boxes on the following page.

- Step 1 Narrowing the list: Review the list of values below. Identify the 12 values that mean the most to you. Cross out the values that are not as important as those 12. (Note: If you added additional values, cross out a sufficient number of values so that only 12 values remain.)

- Step 2: Getting harder...of the 12 remaining values, cross out six additional values, so you now have six remaining.

- Step 3: The last step is to cross out two additional values so that you, through a difficult decision making process, identified four values that are most important to you.

- Step 4: Circle the remaining four values and list them on page 47.

Values

Achievement	Friendship	Continuous learning	Adventure
Service to Others	Being in Charge	Competition	Helping Others
Intellectual Stimulation	Recognition	Status	Helping Society
Serenity	Wealth	Variety	Change
Physical Activity	Working with Others	Fun	Privacy
Religion	Excitement	Family	Challenges

Although it was difficult to eliminate values, in the end the four that remained, that survived the process, are important to consider when you plan your retirement as they represent what is most important to you at this time.

The following are the four most important values to you at this time in your life.

Value 1
....

Value 2
....

Value 3
....

Value 4
....

What additional thoughts do you have about these values that might impact what you choose to do in retirement? Example: One of my top values is helping society. Maybe I can find opportunities where I can use my carpentry skills to help others. I might consider things like helping Habitat for Humanity or volunteer to work in an after school program and teach young people how to build things.

....

....

....

....

....

Now you should be able to summarize what you discovered about yourself that will help you plan for a rewarding retirement.

- *Summary of thoughts: What did you learn about yourself as a result of answering the questions about additional interests, successes, preferences, social needs and the values that are most important to you? Example: I like being a leader and want to find opportunities to use my leadership skills. I need to figure out how to find new friends without getting involved in formal and large organizations*

....

....

....

....

....

- *Conclusion: What three things are you most passionate about? Example: art, travel, tennis, history*

....

....

....

....

....

....

....

....

- *In retirement, which (three to five) strengths/skills that you identified do you want to focus on? Example: Leadership skills, ability to play the piano, financial knowledge*

....

....

....

....

....

....

- *What have you always wanted to do or learn if only you had more time? Example: Learn to play the piano, take a safari in Africa*

....

....

....

....

- *What relationships do you want to strengthen? Example: Grandchildren, aging parents, oldest brother*

....

....

....

....

....

STEP 2: IDENTIFYING ACTIVITY PATHS

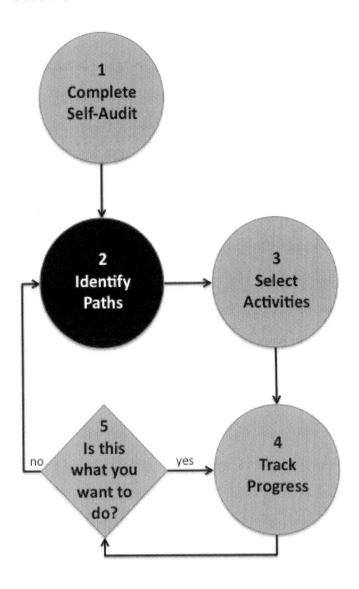

■ STEP 2: IDENTIFYING ACTIVITY PATHS

"The person born with a talent they are meant to use will find their greatest happiness in using it."

- Johann Wolfgang von Goethe

The exercises in "Completing a Self Audit" helped you identify what you like to do, what you are good at doing, and what matters to you. You now have a snapshot of your past and have taken the first steps in thinking about your future.

Many retirees have found that it was rewarding to have a more focused approach to how they spent the majority of their time. They developed paths that consisted of related activities linked together by a common theme. For example, Bob had always been very interested in the Civil War. The path he created consisted of various activities that helped him learn even more about the civil war: visiting at least two battlefields a year, taking a university class on important generals in the war, and starting a book club focused on the Civil War.

Successful retirees often linked their activity paths to their previous profession, something they had been thinking about doing for a long time or something they were passionate about.

They asked themselves questions to help them identify a link between their past and the future.

Retirement Links

Links to...	Questions to Ask
A Previous Profession	Is there a way you can apply your career expertise in a different way? *Example: Retired high school art teacher opens his own art gallery.*
A Passion	What are you passionate about? *Example: Volunteering at an animal shelter.*
A Longtime Desire	What kinds of things have you wanted to do but due to a lack of time, you could not do during your career years? *Example: Become an actor in the local community theater group*

The following pages provide four stories of retirees and their chosen activity paths.

Retiree #1: Mike L

<u>Profession:</u> Technology specialist

<u>Why chose to retire:</u> Work was no longer challenging or rewarding

<u>Chosen Path:</u> Find ways to explore love of music.

Within six months of admitting that his job had changed from fun, challenging and rewarding to drudgery, Mike trained his successor and was out the door.

While he was still working, Mike started to think about retirement. He was concerned that he would be lonely and bored so he came up with a list of activities he would like to do.

But only two years into retirement Mike discovered many new things to do. Some of the things he thought he would like were replaced by new activities that he found more interesting and challenging.

While he enjoyed photography, it did not become a major focus as he had expected. And, he did not like serving as a board member for a nonprofit organization. He felt that it was too much like work, with all the meetings and political positioning.

Mike owns a horse. When Mike was working, he would often ride his horse as a way to reduce his stress. Now in retirement he finds that he rides his horse less.

Mike had played the trumpet in the high school band. He had loved his experience in the band. For four years, he spent five days a week in band class as well as attending concerts and band competitions with the same people. From the quality time they spent together, he and his fellow band members developed lasting relationships. In fact, one of the lasting relationships that came out of his days in the band was with the woman he married. Recently Mike and his wife hosted a band reunion for their previous band leader who was celebrating 50 years of teaching.

Now retired, Mike wanted, in addition to playing the trumpet, the challenge of learning a new instrument – an instrument that had always interested him. So he took lessons and learned how to play the euphonium.

Mike currently plays in two concert bands and is reliving all the enjoyment he had when he played in the high school band.

Retiree #2: Larry F

<u>Profession:</u> University professor

<u>Why chose to retire:</u> Teaching was no longer fun and financially his pension had become equal to what he would get paid if he continued to work.

<u>Chosen Paths:</u> Find new ways to use expertise in new product development, find ways to satisfy desire to build things, continue to help immigrants learn English as a second language and find ways to keep in good physical condition.

Although Larry had tired of teaching, he still wanted to be involved in his field of choice – marketing focused on new product development. Immediately after he retired, Larry got a part-time consulting job writing materials for an online MBA course in marketing.

During his retirement he got the university to adopt a unique revolutionary curriculum he had developed a few years ago. Larry currently visits the campus twice a year to participate in critiquing students' projects. He says that helping students is "the most worthwhile thing I have ever done."

Larry developed empathy for immigrants who struggled to read and speak English. Before retirement, he was a volunteer for a literacy program. Now, he tutors English as a second language, often going to the homes of people who want help.

As well as activities that involve the intellect, Larry likes to build and fix things. His first project after retirement was to design and build a unique garden shed. He continued to help with his son's metalworking business and spent a whole summer remodeling his daughter's condo.

To keep in good physical condition, Larry joined line ball and volleyball teams and even surprised himself when he found out that he indeed had competitive juices.

"Although I didn't give any thought to what I might do after retirement," he said, "I have found many activities that are rewarding. I am comfortable financially, live in a home that I've completely remodeled and have been happily married for almost 52 years. The good health my wife and I enjoy is more than the icing on the cake!"

Retiree #3: Joan Y

Profession: Manager, customer service organization

Why chose to retire: length of employment and a good retirement package

Chosen Path: Find new ways to use passion for clothes, retail business and working with people.

Retirement was something Joan looked forward to for several years. She and her husband, Richard, had planned to take many trips to exotic places all around the world. She looked forward to having time to read all the piles of books waiting on her bookshelf and to spend more time with her friends.

But when Richard died two years and one trip after she retired, Joan sat on her couch trying to figure out how she could get out of the rut in which she found herself.

Joan felt at a loss for how to spend all the free time she now had. She missed the structure provided by her job as well as the camaraderie she had with her team. She took pride in the fact that she was appreciated and valued for her expertise and her success with managing an award-winning customer service organization. Although the job-related stress was at times too much, Joan now realized that it was also energizing.

After about six months of self-pity, Joan decided that she wanted to get a part-time job and went to a career counselor who specialized in helping mature adults find part-time work. The counselor offered Joan two possibilities: reception work in a medical office, or a position as a personal shopper for an upscale department store.

Confused, Joan wondered if either of the jobs would offer anything more than a way to pass the time. Would she feel like she was doing something worthwhile? Would she find fulfillment?

Not knowing what to do, she called her son. He helped her identify what she liked to do and where she excelled. Through the discussion, she discovered that she loves working with people and the fashion industry.

Joan took the personal shopper job that provided opportunities to work in a variety of clothing stores. At 70-plus, Joan finds her work rewarding and likes making a difference in people's lives.

Retiree #4: Karen W

<u>Profession:</u> School district director of media

<u>Why chose to retire:</u> Work was harder and less enjoyable and her husband, Bob, was already retired.

<u>Chosen Path:</u> Find ways to explore love of plants and gardening, find how to use expertise of libraries, and identify ways to use a lifelong passion for farming.

Karen and Bob's exciting retirement plans were thwarted by Bob's health problems. Karen kept herself busy sewing as well as being an advocate for Bob. She spent a lot of time on the computer doing research on available treatment options.

Karen was pleased that her expertise in research was valuable to finding procedures that helped Bob, but she missed the excitement she felt when she had the responsibilities associated with being the person in change of the media department. When Karen was working, she knew that her contributions were valued and she enjoyed the built in social network. Now she felt, however, there was no direction, no structure in her life.

Karen began to think about the things that she liked and were important to her. Having grown up on a farm, she always loved working with plants so the first path she decided to explore was gardening. Not only was working in the yard therapeutic, it gave her the opportunity to grow as she explored how to introduce new plants into her garden, take classes to learn about different plants and attend plant sales.

Karen also found a part-time position that allowed her to use her expertise in libraries. After one of her visits to a library, Karen stopped for coffee and saw an ad for the local Farm Bureau. The ad was looking for someone who had grown up on a farm and wanted to help educate students on farmers and farming. "I'm that person," Karen said.

Karen loves going into the schools and helping the students as well as the teachers learn what is required to get food to your table. The kids see her as a special visitor.

Karen is excited about all three areas: gardening, library assessments and teaching. She feels she is providing value, her life has a focus and she is involved in activities that are challenging and rewarding.

Other Activity Paths Chosen by Retirees

- Expand my music experiences

- Expand my knowledge of art

- Keep mentally challenged

- Do the "fun" things I never had time to do

- Meet new people

- Find new ways to use my financial skills

- Find volunteer opportunities where I can:
    - Work with children...or
    - Support my favorite charity...or
    - Support my favorite museum...or
    - Use my nursing skills...or
    - Share my love for the outdoors...or

On the following page is a form to list the path(s) you would like to follow. A copy-ready blank "Activity Path" form can be found in the Appendix.

Identifying Activity Paths

Paths I would like to take...

Path 1

....

....

....

Path 2

....

....

....

Path 3

....

....

....

Path 4

....

....

....

STEP 3: SELECTING ACTIVITIES

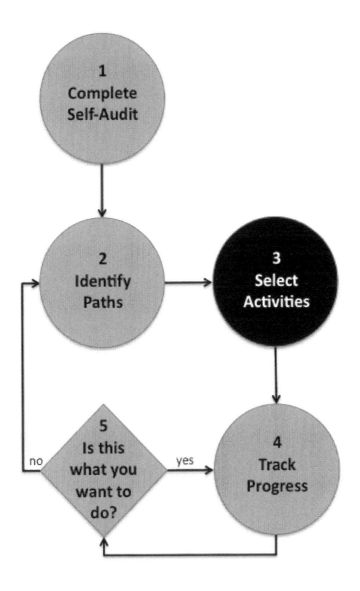

■ STEP 3: SELECTING ACTIVITIES

For each of your selected paths, there are many directions you can take, many different things you can do. For example, say you have chosen a path that involves working with animals. You could volunteer to work at an animal shelter, or you could get a full-time or part-time job working at a zoo. You could plan a trip to Africa to see animals in their natural habitat. You could write a children's book about a special animal in your life – the list goes on. There are two steps to selecting activities:

- Step 1: Use your creativity to compile a list of activities for each path you have identified. Come up with as many ideas as possible. Do not concern yourself with *how* you would do the activity. Think with an open mind.

  You might discuss your path with others to see if they have additional ideas. You should identify at least eight possibilities for each path.

- Step 2: Select three to five of the ideas that you think would be rewarding and/or enjoyable and list them in the Activities to Explore area on the form.

On the following pages are two lists of sample paths, and for each path:

- An extensive list of activities to consider.
- A modified list of activities worth exploring.

Following the two sample paths plus activities there is a form to help you identify activities you could do to support your chosen path(s). A copy ready blank "Selecting Activities" form can be found in the Appendix.

SAMPLE: Selecting Activities

Path

Expand on my love of art

....

Brainstorm Possible Activities

Take a variety of classes to explore different kinds of art
....
Work in an art gallery
....
Find a travel program that focuses on art museums
....
Get a part-time job or volunteer at an art museum
....
Run an art program in a childrens' summer camp
....
Become involved in providing art therapy
....
Volunteer to conduct art programs for children with
learning disabilities
....
Take an art class at a university outside the United States
....

Activities to Explore

Take a variety of classes to explore different kinds of art
....
Get a part-time job or volunteer at an art museum
....
Volunteer to conduct art programs for children with
learning disabilities
....

....

....

....

SAMPLE: Selecting Activities

Path

Find ways to use my financial expertise

....

....

Brainstorm Possible Activities

Volunteer to help a favorite charity
....
Teach finance courses in a junior college
....
Get a part-time job during tax preparation season
....
Volunteer to help senior citizens with finances
....
Tutor/mentor students
....
Write a book on finances
....
Volunteer to work for SCORE (Service Corp of Retired Executives)
....
Develop and deliver to a non-profit organization (e.g. church or senior center) a presentation on tax saving tips
....

....

Activities to Explore

Volunteer to help the American Cancer Society
....
Volunteer to help senior citizens with finances
....
Volunteer to work for SCORE
....

....

....

....

Selectng Activities

Path

....

....

Brainstorm Possible Activities

....

....

....

....

....

....

....

....

....

Activities to Explore

....

....

....

....

....

Important Check Point

Assuming that you selected paths and activities that are based on what you like to do, what you are good at and what is important to you, - review the activities you selected to see if they will replace the positive aspects (social networks, self-worth and structure) of the workplace.

If the activities you identified will not help you replace what you had in the workplace, then modify some of the activities or idenify new ones.

Two sample Check Point Forms have been provided. A copy-ready blank "Check Point: Rating the Activities" form can be found in the Appendix.

Check Point: Rating the Activities

Path: Find ways to use my financial expertise.

On a scale of 1 to 5 (with 1 being not supportive and 5 being very supportive), rate each activity as to what extent it helps replace the positive aspects of the workplace.

Activity	Structure	Social Network	Self-Worth
Volunteer to provide financial assistance to a favorite charity	4	3	5
Volunteer to work for SCORE	5	5	5
Teach finance courses in Junior College	5	5	5
Get a part-time job during tax preparation season	5	3	5

Check Point: Rating the Activities

SAMPLE B

Path: Expand on my love of art.

On a scale of 1 to 5 (with 1 being not supportive and 5 being very supportive), rate each activity as to what extent it helps replace the positive aspects of the workplace.

Activity	Structure	Social Network	Self-Worth
Take several art classes to explore different aspects of art I am not familiar with (Note: This activity although not highly rated, could lead to the identification of additional activities.)	2	2	3
Get a part-time job or volunteer at an art museum	5	5	4
Find a travel program that focuses on art	4	5	3
Volunteer to conduct art programs for children with learning disabilities	5	5	5

Check Point: Rating the Activities

Path:

On a scale of 1 to 5 (with 1 being not supportive and 5 being very supportive), rate each activity as to what extent it helps replace the positive aspects of the workplace.

Activity	Structure	Social Network	Self-Worth

STEP 4: TRACK PROGRESS

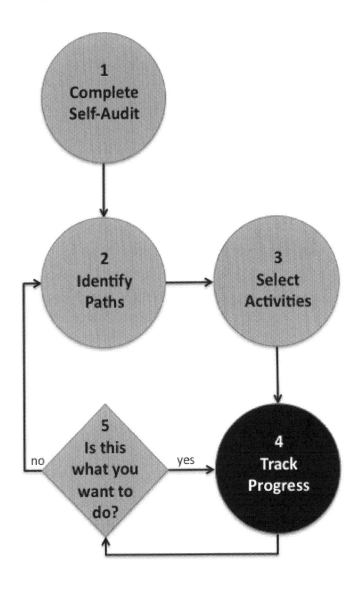

■ STEP 4: TRACK PROGRESS

Tracking your progress is critical if you want to achieve your goals.

Studies have shown that people working on projects do better when they keep track of their progress.

In the business world a variety of methods are used to ensure goals will be achieved. Progress is assessed by using project plans, review meetings as well as written and verbal reports.

Tracking also gives you the opportunity to see potential challenges that might hamper goals from being achieved and make adjustments .

The following pages provide samples of two informal tracking reports. In each exercise an accomplishment (positive or negative) should lead to a follow-up action.

A blank copy-ready "Tracking Progress" form can be found in the Appendix.

Tracking Progress

Path	Expand love of literature
Activity	Become a storyteller
Initial Steps	▪ Find/attend a storytelling class ▪ Find/join storytelling organization ▪ Research to find possible audiences

Progress	Next Steps
1/11: Took class, joined librarian group, need to make decision; deliver stories to adults or children, find initial audience, identify appropriate stories, deliver program and evaluate success.	▪ Review adult and children's stories to see which ones are more appealing. ▪ Visit a storytelling performance for adults and a storytelling performance for children. ▪ Discuss with storytelling class teacher.
3/9: Decided to deliver stories to senior citizen groups.	▪ Research to find appropriate short stories. ▪ Master delivery of selected stories. ▪ Select location. ▪ Make arrangements. ▪ Deliver program/evaluate.
12/1: Have conducted several programs. Good reviews. Have been asked to conduct more programs, so I need to expand repertoire.	Meet with storytelling teacher to review sources for stories appropriate for senior citizens.

Tracking Progress

Path:	Participate in competitive activities
Activity:	Learn to play bridge
Initial Steps:	<ul><li>Find/attend a bridge class</li><li>Call Bill to learn about the bridge group he belongs to</li><li>Call the local Senior Center to see if it has bridge groups for beginners</li><li>Check local newspaper and library to find other possible groups</li></ul>

Progress	Next Steps
5/6: Took class. Observed Bill's group; decided it was too advanced.	<ul><li>Locate/attend beginners group at the Senior Center.</li><li>Identify group in local newspaper.</li></ul>
7/8: Group at Senior Center too advanced. Took another beginner's class with different teacher. Better results. I understand the game better. Attended two sessions with local group. Seems like a good place to start.	<ul><li>Evaluate appropriateness of group in four to six months.</li><li>Take more lessons, if necessary.</li><li>Find ways to practice skills, e.g., Internet sites and daily newspapers.</li></ul>

Tracking Progress

Path:	
Activity:	
Initial Steps:	

Progress	Next Steps

STEP 5: MONITORING SUCCESS

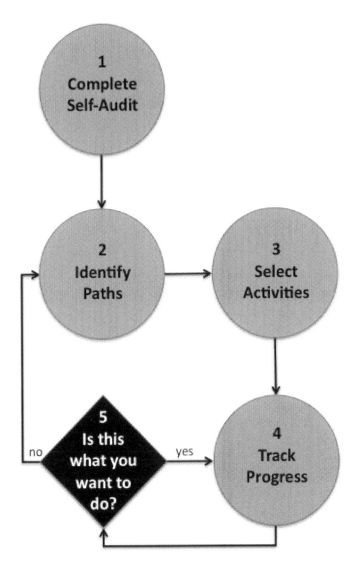

■ STEP 5: MONITORING SUCCESS

Studies have shown that in the workplace, employees who desire to be successful want feedback from their managers. They like to know how they are performing and how they can improve their performance. High-performance companies have formal programs that provide employees with measurement goals and frequent feedback on how they are performing in meeting their goals.

Frequent feedback that includes progress made on goals provides confirmation that the employee is making sufficient progress or not. If not, adjustments can be made so that the employee can successfully meet the goals by the due date.

In previous sections, by identifying paths of interests and supporting activities, you have established a list of goals you wish to accomplish.

Like business goals, the chance for achieving a satisfying retirement is increased when progress is monitored and when necessary modifications are made .

Monitoring the progress of your retirement plans should be ongoing, and you should review your plans and make modifications often. You might change your mind about what you like and what you dislike as you experience new things and meet new people. With your new freedom, you must ensure you are doing things and having experiences that are fulfilling.

On the following pages are questions to help you assess the life you have built for yourself. A blank copy-ready "Assessment" form can be found in the Appendix.

Assessing Retirement Expectations

1. Assessment of Paths and Activities	
Questions	**Comments**
Am I satisfied with the Activity Paths I have chosen? If not, which ones need to be changed? What new paths should I explore?	
What activities have I liked doing and what activities have I not liked doing?	
Based on what I have been doing and the knowledge and experience I have gained, are there activities I should add or delete?	
Were there any activities that might work better if I implemented them differently?	
Based on what I have done since the last review of my activities, did I discover any new information that might change how I am spending my time? e.g., In addition to my volunteer work, I would like to get a paying part-time job.	

2. General Assessment

Questions	Comments
Social interaction and physical activities are important for maintaining good physical and mental health. Are there additional social and/or physical activities I should consider?	
Do I have enough structure to meet my needs? (Too little structure can result in boredom and negative feelings while being overly structured can result in a lack of flexibility and increased stress level.)	
Do I still miss work? If the answer is yes, then what am I missing? What additional activities should I consider?	
Am I just keeping busy or are my activities organized into paths that create a planned, diligent approach to building a satisfying retirement?	

3. Other Questions

Questions	Comments

APPENDIX

- **The Four Keys to Crafting a Successful Retirement**

- **Copy-Ready Blank Forms**

■ The Four Keys to Crafting a Successful Retirement

■ Key #1

Can I afford to retire?

During your working career, your employer provided you with a paycheck. Guess what? After retirement, you will still want to take a trip, buy groceries, go to the movies and buy new clothes. But there will be no company paycheck coming in on a regular basis.

You might wonder if you can afford to retire. The answer is "yes," if there is a balance between the income you will generate in retirement and the anticipated annual expenses.

Total
Income   *Total*
                                              Expenses

Total income = Amount of anticipated income from Social Security (minus Medicare costs) plus any annuities or fixed pensions plus income from other retirement funds

Expenses = Total amount required to maintain desired lifestyle

Many of the retirees I talked to were concerned they didn't have the financial means to retire. However, once they met with a professional financial adviser, they were able to see a path to retirement.

What if I don't have a balance between my total income and my expected expenses?

It is best to identify your retirement goals and create a supportive financial plan about five years before your ideal retirement date.

When you put your total anticipated income and expected expenses side by side, there might not be a balance. You might find you do not have enough anticipated income to cover your expected expenses.

To achieve a balance, you need to first figure out the difference between what income you will have to spend and what you need to maintain your desired lifestyle.

After reviewing the numbers you might need to make some difficult choices. You might need to increase your income or reduce your expenses to achieve a balance between what funds you need and have.

Increase Funds	Reduce Expenses (Prior to and During Retirement)
In retirement find a new full-time or part-time job that will generate enough money to create a balance between income and expenses.	Reduce the number of trips you take and/or or select lower-cost travel destinations.
Rebalance your retirement funds so that you have additional income producing products.	Prior to retirement pay off large expenses (e.g, a home mortgage or car loan).
Take a second job prior to retirement to increase your retirement fund.	Buy a car and do home repairs prior to retirement.
	Reduce the amount you plan to spend on discretionary items (e.g,. buy less expensive camera, purchase less clothing, buy paperback books or use the library, do your own lawn work).
	Find low-cost programs offered to seniors instead of expensive university programs.
	Sell home and buy smaller, less expensive home.
	Do not purchase vacation home.

■ Key #2

Free Time in Retirement

> If you have goals and procrastinate, you will have nothing. If you have goals and you take action, you will have anything you want.
>
> - Thomas J. Vilord

It is quite different trying to fill the relatively small amount of time you have away from work responsibilities vs. coming up with ideas to fill all the days and evenings for the rest of your life.

It is Monday morning, I finished breakfast, checked email, surfed the Internet, and took a shower after spending an hour on the treadmill. I look at the clock. It is only 10:30 am.

I sit down at the kitchen table and think: "So, what should I do today?"

Choices:

- Clean the shower stall.

- Go to the card store to buy a birthday card for my daughter.

- Finish the book I have been reading.

- Call my friend to find out how her visit to the doctor went.

- Go through medical documentation to see what still needs to be paid.

- Watch television.

Actually, on most days I would have time to do all six activities and more.

However, without a well-thoughtout plan, the days can go by and nothing gets accomplished. Retirees who idle away their time are the ones who say they do not like retirement. When asked, they say retirement is boring and encourage others to work for as long as they can.

One key to enjoying your retirement years is to create a weekly plan and set daily goals, which provide you structure. Your plan and goals do not have to be formal. They don't even have to be written down. The goal for one day could be to spend the whole day reading!

Create a Weekly Schedule

Based on scheduled activities already on my calendar, such as doctor appointments or attending the weekly bridge club, I determine how much time I can devote to working on activities. Maybe it is a week when I have several appointments and social activities. That week I might just do one small activity to ensure that I feel like I am making progress on my goals. Other weeks I might have lots of unscheduled time. Those are the weeks to identify activities that require a good deal of time, e.g. going through paperwork that is linked to old tax returns.

Since I am creating the goals and I am the one who decides how I'm going to spend my time, I have flexibility. I can make whatever changes I want. Sometimes I am not in the mood to do an activity. For example, maybe on Wednesday I planned to go through old tax return files but decided that this is not a time when I want to sit at a desk and go through paperwork. Instead I could throw out all the old paint cans in the basement. Or, maybe I will decide to take a day off and play golf.

Create Daily Goals

Before I get out of bed each morning, I select two to three things I want to accomplish by the time I go back to bed.

The daily goals can be simple, such as pulling out plants that were destroyed by the frost or making a phone call to a friend who just got out of the hospital. As appropriate, I include chosen path and project activities into my daily goals. If I was working on "Reducing the Clutter in my Life," one for the daily goals could be to go through the bookcases in the den and find at least ten books which I can donate to the local veteran's hospital.

Some days I will have completed simple goals. On other days I will have completed important or perhaps complex goals. Or, I might have a mixture – some simple and some complex.

■ Key #3

Rebuilding Your Social Network

"Research shows that routine socialization is one of the key aspects of successful aging, so it's important for seniors to find social activities."

- Mary Hujer

With more and more Baby Boomers approaching retirement, there is an increased interest in understanding the role of socialization later in life.

Research shows that older adults who have strong social networks seem to have a higher quality of life, live longer and are healthier compared to those with little social support (Glass, Mendes de Leon, Marottolie & Berkman, 1999). Also, studies show that strong social support seems to protect against cognitive decline and self-reported disability (Mendes de Leon, Glass, & Berkman, 2003).

The workplace provides opportunities for informal and formal social networking. Retirees miss their work relationships and the sense of belonging that was a natural outgrowth of working with others. They miss the opportunity for shared experiences. For example, engineers are motivated and challenged by working with other engineers. Natural conversations develop around work-related issues. Sometimes it's sharing a team success or trying to understand the boss' decision that everyone turn in a weekly work report or discussing why your company will merge with another company. Seeing each other on a regular basis also builds friendships that provide support when someone is having a good experience (son's wedding) or a bad experience (losing a mate).

Without the easy access the workplace provides for social interaction, retirees have to rebuild their social world.

When you completed the activities in this book, you had the opportunity to identify what types of social activities best meet your needs.

If you discovered that you are someone who likes being part of a group, there are almost unlimited opportunities. Many senior centers, as well as libraries, places of worship, junior colleges and universities provide programs.

There also are opportunities to join groups based on your interests, such as golf, tennis, bridge, reading, or playing an instrument.

For those who like being part of a group, the challenge is to figure out what interests you and to find a group that focuses on your interest. However, if you, like me, do not find satisfaction in being part of a group, there are other paths to follow.

Rather than having many acquaintances, I prefer having a few good friends. Much of my social interactions are spent with my small circle of friends. Since we share common interests, it is easy to come up with things to do together, such as going to a concert, visiting the botanical gardens, going to a ballgame, or having a nice dinner together .

Research shows that it is critical that you rebuild your social network. You need to identify your social preferences and plan accordingly - whether it is to find appropriate group activities, or to build a small group of quality friendships, or both.

By being socially connected, you are more likely to have a fulfilling retirement and a healthy life to enjoy!

■ Key #4

Volunteering

Want to build social networks, self-worth and structure quickly and easily? Volunteer!

Using what you learned about yourself by going through the activities in the book, you should be able to identify a volunteering opportunity that will give you the chance to meet new people, make a difference in the lives of others and help add definition to your life. It will help replace the things you miss about the workplace.

Volunteering provides many rewards. It provides opportunities to:

1. Grow and learn more about yourself as well as discover new skills and capabilities.

2. Help others, which provides you a sense of joy, self-satisfaction and value.

3. Give back to the community.

4. Connect with other people who share your passions.

5. Engage in new, enriching and possibly exciting experiences.

6. Build self-esteem.

7. Feel a sense of accomplishment from getting things done.

8. Engage in challenging activities.

9. Spend time on your passions.

10. Enjoy!

There are many ways to find volunteering opportunities based on what you like to do and what you are good at doing. The Internet offers many websites devoted to identifying volunteering opportunities. I found volunteering opportunities on www.volunteermatch.org.

How much time you spend volunteering depends upon you and your schedule. I know someone who works in a school every afternoon of the week. I prefer more free time, so I volunteer once a week and offer a second day if my schedule permits.

Find a situation that seems to match what you are looking for. Try it for a period of time. Communicate on a regular basis with the people who are supporting your volunteer efforts. Let them know what is working and what is not working so that they can make adjustments.

If after a period of time you either discover a better opportunity or realize you don't like what you are doing, search for another place to offer your expertise.

Being a volunteer can give you as much - if not more - than it gives the people, places or animals you choose to help.

■ COPY-READY BLANK FORMS

Identifying Activity Paths

Paths I would like to take...

Path 1

....

....

....

Path 2

....

....

....

Path 3

....

....

....

Path 4

....

....

....

Selecting Activities

Path

....

....

Brainstorm Possible Activities

....

....

....

....

....

....

....

....

Activities to Explore

....

....

....

....

....

Check Point: Rating the Activities

Path:

On a scale of 1 to 5 (with 1 being not supportive and 5 being very supportive), rate each activity as to what extent it helps replace the positive aspects of the workplace.

Activity	Structure	Social Network	Self-Worth

Tracking Progress

Path:	
Activity:	
Initial Steps:	

Progress	Next Steps

Assessing Retirement Expectations

1. Assessment of Paths and Activities	
Questions	**Comments**
Am I satisfied with the Activity Paths I have chosen? If not, which ones need to be changed? What new paths should I explore?	
What activities have I liked doing and what activities have I not liked doing?	
Based on what I have been doing and the knowledge and experience I have gained, are there activities I should add or delete?	
Were there any activities that might work better if I implemented them differently?	
Based on what I have done since my last review of my activities, did I discover any new information that might change how I am spending my time? e.g., In addition to my volunteer work, I would like to get a paying part-time job.	

2. General Assessment

Questions	Comments
Social interaction and physical activities are important for maintaining good physical and mental health. Are there additional social and/or physical activities I should consider?	
Do I have enough structure to meet my needs? (Too little structure can result in boredom and negative feelings while being overly structured can result in a lack of flexibility and increased stress level.)	
Do I still miss work? If the answer is yes, then what am I missing? What additional activities should I consider?	
Am I just keeping busy or are my activities organized into paths that create a planned, diligent approach to building a satisfying retirement?	

3. Other Questions

Questions	Comments

"Each sunrise gives hope to your dreams and light to your plans."

- William Ngwako Maphoto

Made in the USA
San Bernardino, CA
21 February 2019